Escape from Prison

Escape *from* Prison

Mary Ngwebong Ngu

Spears Books

Spears Books
An Imprint of Spears Media Press LLC
7830 W. Alameda Ave, Suite 103-247
Denver, CO 80226
United States of America

First Published in the United States of America in 2021 by Spears Books
www.spearsmedia.com
info@spearsmedia.com
@spearsbooks

Information on this title: www.spearsmedia.com/escape-from-prison

ISBN: 9781942876861 (Paperback)
ISBN: 9781942876878 (eBook)
Also available in Kindle format

Artwork credits:
Initial sketch on cover art, and images introducing Parts 1, 2, 3, 4 and partially 5
(modified by author): Frank Prince Garriba
"Pining for a Special Guest": Fontoh Philemon
"A Dream Come True" & finalizing the cover art: Bright Toh
"Sitting on the Fence": author

Cover designed by DK
Designed and typeset by Spears Media Press LLC

Distributed globally by African Books Collective (ABC)
www.africanbookscollective.com

To you in jail, detained or parading the streets
In politico-socio-economic, or spiritual chains.
To you in pain, chained by tragic personal circumstances
Though armed with freewill.
To you, physically and emotionally challenged,
Yet determined to topple the dire straits.
May you keep hope alive to tip the scales at last,
In time to catch the train
To arrive the mill!

CONTENTS

FOREWORD

Mary first caught my attention when she was going through a personal life crisis. The wonderful romance of her marriage had turned sour. Beyond my remote involvement as a lawyer, I could feel the pain of the parties involved. She subsequently travelled to the United States of America, and although I could not help empathizing with her, this journey must have healed her. Not only was I happy for her, but she remained a reference. This book is concrete proof.

Her collection of poems, written while in detention, attests to the resilience of a woman who has been through pain but has not allowed it to destroy her. On the contrary, she has been able to overcome, to transcend herself, to the extent of encouraging others through her writing. Take a look at the various themes that permeate *Escape from Prison*. They cover the whole gamut of internal struggles in time of trouble. The causes of misfortunes be they direct or indirect, and the ensuing complications have significant ramifications for human relationships at multiple levels.

Thus, the questions that this collection provokes address themselves to everyone in society. What is the impact of our decisions and actions on the lives of others, whether they be informal or accruing from the use or misuse of the power conferred upon us by our offices? Ultimately, the question is, what is the contribution of each person in adopting measures as well as building societal structures aimed at forestalling future calamities, especially those that destabilize families, directly affecting children and worsening the situation of the vulnerable?

Whatever our answers, a collection of poems wherein the author bares her soul in a scholarly manner, yet one that can be grasped by anyone beyond the literati, is an awesome gift to her community, both in her hometown in Cameroon, the USA (scene of the culmination of events depicted), and the world at large. The overall therapeutic effect of this collection on the reader is outstanding: Mary's expression of pain, rather than plunging her and her readers into depression, flings open windows of hope. Similarly, her gentle sense of humour creates the opportunity for her listeners or readers to introspect, with the inclination to confront the often or outrightly neglected frontiers that should eventually create more cohesion in society.

I am delighted for this opportunity to introduce Mary Ngwebong Ngu to you through the brilliant creativity of her mind as expressed in *Escape from Prison*.

Ephraim Ngwafor, *Professor of Law*

PREFACE

I arrived in the USA on the 11th of September 1993, on the sponsorship of the United States Information Service (USIS) to take part in the Young African Leaders program. Unbeknown to the organisers, honoring their invitation was a way of fleeing from life-threatening domestic violence. At the end of our stay, I found myself in a quandary. More complications arose with time until I was arrested and thrown into jail.

Prior to my incarceration, I had been writing poetry, having published my first collection in 2001, two years before I was arrested. However, my previous writing was a leisure activity on a variety of themes, from relationships to life in society. Suddenly losing my personal freedom left me in shock. It drowned me in painful thoughts, recent and remote that were gnawing away at my innate joy. Incapacitating circumstances notwithstanding, I had an advantage that I had never had since childhood—time.

On the second morning, I was drained; depleted of energy due to crying. I missed my diary badly so, I bought a pen and a notebook. Instead of merely noting what had happened, I had a need to elaborate. I wrote the first three lines, recapturing the moment of my arrest. Then I paused and read over. They sounded coherent. So, I kept on until I finished the first stanza, then the second and the third. On the spur of the moment, I realised that my attention had shifted from myself to include others.

Later, I shared my poem with a few friends in the yard during our evening encounter. Each of them grabbed it, read it with remarkable attention, and made comments, while expressing their desire for more. Right there, they started sharing information about themselves, especially why they were in jail. Two of them told me that they were poets too.

The following evening, I brought a freshly written poem. The other poets each had a poem, including another young lady who was inspired. We read each other's poems, asked questions, and critiqued them. Our exchange soon became a poetry club meeting behind bars; and more were joining. After each session, I returned to my cell and edited my poem.

It was the first time that I was using art to express pain. The more ideas I had, the more key episodes in my life came to mind. I began experiencing a novel type of freedom or was it a courage or need —to share my pain with others. Not until that moment, did I realise the therapeutic power of confronting one's pain as a means of seeking healing, especially when I tried to put myself in the place of others in similar circumstances, including those who had contributed to my hurt.

Henceforth, I was spending most of my time writing, as if I had been locked up with the sole purpose of obliging me to confront the string of pent-up anguish from multiple crises that had been devasting in several ways, rendering me helpless. Now you understand how I came about the title, *Escape from Prison.*

Hopefully, these poems, whose themes run from resilience, moral values, human relationships, deception, betrayal, coping with estrangement from family, suffering, life in jail, systemic hurdles to progress, to surviving in a foreign land, would motivate readers to avoid entangling pitfalls, while working to overcome restrictions to development, self-imposed or external.

PART 1

THE ARREST: HOW AND WHY

Arrested By Fear

The prosecutor pointed at me, leveling accusations
Causing lurking Mister Fear to grip me tightly
Of course, he had been analyzing my phobia breath by breath
Closely following the proceedings of tarnishing tales
Rising and spiraling like dust particles blinding my vision
Imaginary accounts composed to sound like a crime
Detonating itsy-bitsy bombs to induce tremors in my being
Silencing my cry for mercy in the high place of State

Strong muscles escorted the criminal they labeled me
While sly Miss Apprehension provoked heart-quakes
My heartbeat raced, feet trembled,
Eyes blinded by gushing tears
Attacking my faith in the system:
Error or racist-xenophobic incarceration?
Subjected to gusts of rushing waves
Amidst advancing tempests
The deluge of harsh words drowned my exhausted nerves
Hurling my self-esteem into ghastly gutters
Of multilingual muggers
My shocked veins swelled,
Documenting my doom for the record

In the speedy van, I curtseyed
To the attending Miss Nightmare
Gush! why didn't Professor Pedigree grant me extra time
To pack my stuff, bid farewell, and quit with dignity?
Weren't most of today's citizens
And personalities yesterday's aliens?
My investments ruined, plans marred, contracts abandoned
The packer blade of the garbage truck
Compressed my ambition into a trash
I became a punching bag in a hellhole

With charges splitting my hairs
The sudden arrest was wanton aggression

Arriving at the fenced compound,
I cried out, "alas, Dr. Dread!"
Officers admitting a victim
In the precinct of the busy jailhouse,
As a thug condemned
For invading dark streets, causing distress
The traumatizing giant, Dr. Dread,
Caught me into a lonely snare
Devouring my energy,
Bleating like a bear, leaping like a leopard,
Trapped, I submitted like a lamb as I kneeled in my cold cell
Praying the lion would pounce
On the awful beasts bullying me
Demeaning looks and tall orders
Reduced me to a mere number
Feeling kidnapped, for how long would I remain unbroken?
Clueless.

A Beacon of Hope

News of the granting of a novel status swelled my heart
My decade-long chance was knocking, I was persuaded
I began reorganizing my life in readiness to receive the license
To relocate to a noble abode
Where all my talents would crop up
I could not help visualizing Canaan barely a few steps away
Imagining the cardinal points of my next settlement

Tired of being tied up as logs,
Drying up and smoldering relentlessly
The new package was the befitting prize of my sacrifice
Farewell to blue-collar jobs with perpetual enslaving orders
No more enervating overtimes in the after hours
I sprinted, my body agile, alert like a skillful athlete
My mind scanning through new professional skills to acquire

Not until I was processed at the counter,
Did I see the accusing looks
Staring into my dismayed countenance?
Only then did I realize I had misinterpreted the convocation
It was too late to heed the warnings of connoisseurs
That had sniffed the smoky flavor
Of sweet poison in my invitation
My spirit sank, unable to release a body caught in a trap
Found wanting on the balance, my freedom was curtailed

I implored the officers to give me a hearing,
But they were deaf, treating me like a crook
Caught in the hook
Thereby forfeiting the chance of humanizing their practice.
Where was their sense of curiosity in passing judgment?
They bypassed the chance to find out
Why a compliant woman disobeyed

The official censure, so tragic,
Reduced authorities to mere robots
Packaging fellow humans like cans
Ready for stacking in the warehouse

Facing a rude awakening,
The plot in the making was no mean gesture
My hopes diminished
While I yearned for a tinge of compassion
They led me through the narrow door
Of sanction within gigantic walls
My being ached and groaned till my voice cracked in plea

Inhibiting commands boggled my befuddled mind
Acknowledging the pig in the poke,
I quickly dismissed my vain hope
Even then, I was still convinced
That the immigration laws were wanting
Humanely speaking,
They desperately needed judicious revision
An extra clause
To treat life-threatening personal stories as exceptions.

No Advocate, No Mercy

I dared to appear in court solo!
Trusting only on my sworn statement in self-defense
Hoping to convince the court of a bygone saga in alien lands
Without the plea of a clever lawyer
Advancing a studied case, testifying,
And proving without doubt
Not so much my innocence,
As the extenuating circumstances
Asphyxiating me
Hindering the fulfilment of heaven's duty of motherhood

Naively I, treaded gingerly towards the judge
Without counsel!
Imagining I could be acquitted
By raising petitioning hands without Johnnie Cochran gloves
When exclusively immigration lawyers
Have eyes that read between the lines of convocations
Skillfully speaking in tongues, deciphering the facts
That I presumed to know without initiation into legal lingo
Laughable in the august presence of both jury and judge

Doggedly I advanced to face judgment
Relying on my innocence for clemency
Trusting in the reign of humanity
In the bosom of the tribunal
Seeking to be trusted though an alien
Venturing to withstand the state's attorney
When only defense lawyers analyze and debunk injunctions
Issued by the prosecutor
Demanding calculated counsel
To answer charges levied with menaces
Like lightning preceding thunder
Is the fatal warning that escaped my prudence

Having mustered up courage to attempt self-defense
Instant condemnation was my lot for defaulting
Not so much in violation of the cited law
As for the lack of respect for the golden rule
That demands the winning argument
Of a hotshot advocate
Pleading for mercy on my behalf.

Does A Statesman Lie?

He intended to bare his soul to his people on the matter
Nothing short of taking the highway
To reach out to fellow citizens
But advisers proposed an odd bill,
A smokescreen touting racial equality
Their justification? - politics is a game of double-edged swords
Each side intentionally employed to suit the target audience
The public blade
Addressing itself to the heterogeneous masses
The private one
Strictly reserved for those behind closed doors

Even his speechwriter refused to edit his piece
Displaying the fascinating version that experts had composed
A bald-faced lie that instantly produced wrinkles on his face
But political pundits praised it
As effective communication management
Couched in bureaucratic jargon:
To camouflage, hypnotize, and mesmerize
For speeches with double interpretations
Are tales dressed in priestly garbs
Turning "status regularization"
In the case of refugees fleeing dungeons
Into "nothing but immediate deportation"
At the dying minute

The matter-of-fact tone of leaders in the heat of a crisis
Sounding steady, yet reversible like the changing weather
Is in line with carefully crafted messages
For mass media broadcasts
Rendering a President's smile
In front of tv cameras a nice façade
Of a double face hard for personalities of the fourth power

To interpret without digging up facts
From classified documents
To irrefutably demonstrate that the President has lied

For indeed, only a statesman, and not a conformist president
Resolutely decides long before his or her inaugural
To eschew the advice of philosophers
Driven by tyrannical governance
A rare courage, involving risking even life, to shun lying
Thus, upholding transparency for the sake of statesmanship.

Blindfolded

I was ushered onto the stage aglow with spotlights
Confidently, I proceeded to declare my innocence
Expecting the instant granting of emancipation
The dying minute lottery vying for my grab
What a chance to revoke my worth!

I spoke up with perfect composure
In a little while,
I would have easy access to rivers of milk and honey
Didn't the law-abiding citizen I was deserve recognition?
After toiling at shop floors, nursing homes, and basements
I even wore a wig for the first time ever
To signal the turning point
In advance of the joyfulness reserved for those who laugh last

After the thunder of applause
The stage director called for assistance
Immediately, I imagined my reward colossal
Instead, there was an unexpected twist in the story
Wherein I became the object of an unfolding drama
Orchestrated for heightened effect

The assistant's hands were clenching a pair of grey cuffs
"Busted," voices howled at me, announcing the climax
On the spot, I perceived pitch darkness
Blotting out the brilliance
Or was it a refining fire?
Whatever, I screamed at the appalling turn of events

Quickly I dried my tears to grapple with the sudden change
How could I be freezing in the heat?
Or was it the harshness of a severe winter?
I strained my eyes to read the thermometer

Were the highlighted numbers pluses or minuses?
Was I facing temptation or taking a test?
Was my lot mere survival or a timely revival?
No, no, it was an invitation to crack tough nuts
But just how could I without the beak of a nutcracker?

Offstage, my heart went on pining without resolve
Right into the commencement of the denouement
During the flashback,
I couldn't help wondering how abruptly, unexpectedly
I had lost my lines
While convulsing before my changing fortune,
Having missed the mark, I was subjected to tattoo piercings
Even right through the exit,
I still hoped it had only been a hallucination
Finally, and bitterly, I admitted that I was blindfolded.

Don't Bury My Talents

They advised me to sign up and earn some quick bucks
At the nursing home
Instead, I began thinking about my parents
And ailing relatives back home
Then they tried to coax me into studying to become a nurse
But how could I dump my certificates
Into the trash like a torn purse?
So, they persuaded me, saying my pay would fill a whole bank
I retorted, refusing to become stale water stored in a tank
Next, they pressurized me into hiring an immigration lawyer
But my defense was impossible
Even to a seasoned dangerous-case portrayer
Since there was no evidence
To show proof of political persecution,
The only option before me
Was the composition of a concoction
Straight away, the red lights began signaling
With me at the steering
Yet they urged me to accelerate
And drive through while they were cheering
Ngang*, ngang, ngang, I cringed
In the face of such a deadly risk
Why should I be reduced to a broken egg
Passing through a whisk?

All these entreaties were intended to ensure my protection
But bent on securing peace of mind, I opted out in rejection
Better to earn a few dollars using my talents,
Dying with my spirit intact
Than to live dishonestly,
Unable to state what I know for a fact

Though simply exercising my freewill, they called me a moron
Insisting I was a nervous wreck,
succumbing to a super active neuron
"Stop the name-calling, the buck stops here,"
I pleaded like a matron
As an immigrant I was richly endowed and experienced
To become a patron
Back in my home country,
Most of my colleagues called me "patron"

Ngang is "no" in Ngemba.

PART 2

DEALING WITH CONFINEMENT

When Is When Enough?

Wasn't it enough
That he broke my heart with induced disaffection?
Wasn't it enough
That a homewrecker considered herself
More deserving of my legacy?
Wasn't it enough
That horror ripped off my children from my nipple?
Wasn't it enough
That I became an IDP, sneaking from house to house?
Wasn't it enough that the judge downplayed my scars?
Wasn't it enough that I forsook my métier for safety's sake?
Wasn't it enough to be disconnected from my social network?
Wasn't it enough
That I wandered far away from my pining family?
Wasn't it enough
To toss out my treasure like trash to hang onto life?
Wasn't it enough
To become a fugitive in a country
Without the notion of shelters?
Wasn't it enough
To tell the truth to get sympathy
From a foreign host government?

Despite all my attempts to migrate like a bird
Caught unawares by violent elements
While in search of a sanctuary
The overpowering forces turned me into a game bird

Having lost all my gains
Secured from the land of milk and honey
Which other baptisms of fire await me after my sentence?
When will the rising flaming fires
Of my life burn enough into ash?

When? Just when is enough?

Surrender

An acquiescing moment on bended knees
For momentum to soar
Forsaking phobia, outrage, self-pity,
And social contaminations
Minding my business when tempted
To gape at the blunders of mates
Keeping faith alive in the face of correctional impediments
Delving into living words in sync with the Master injunction
Striving to practice transforming counsel
Which I have professed

God forbid I exit without investing
In this nadir of my existence
Otherwise, regrettably, irrecoverably, I would be obliged,
And degraded to face stinking,
Stunting assaults, and mugging
More exacerbating than doing time under lock and key
Akin to colliding with daggers drawn, taking me unawares
Like street corner strikes by disguised thugs
A harsh price to pay for ruining submission time

Compelled to dispel aches and regrets
Nibbling away at my investments
Diligently noting dreams and visions worth recounting
Using prolonged muteness to upgrade a weird dwelling
Glazing talents and testimonies to validate my internment
Joining forces with fellow inmates
Wishing to graduate as tough cookies
Sharing a word of comfort
With acquaintances within my purview
Leaning on the robust at recreation in this desert arena

Taking advantage of my raison d'être in this numbing pit
Using mind-mapping during visits
To the in-house make-do library
While conjuring up ginger, *njangsa**,
Mango, and coconut fragrances
To spice up evening promenades
During chatting time in the zephyr
To ease multiple pressures,
Passing for a smiling baby in the creche
Harnessing ideas to stitch together broken pieces of life
To heal the wounds of a soldier maimed in the battle of life.

Njangsa is a tropical oily grain with a pungent odor used to spice and thicken soups

Now

Now is critical
Crucial to existence
As tiny as a pinhead
Yet bearing the stuff
The essence of its worth
To register the signals of the moment
Releasing the breath of lifelines
For status upgrading, linking earth to heaven
Leaving its imprint on the fabric of life
To benefit generations to come
On whose profession and cohesion, the future depends
Thanks to the mettle to withstand the heat
The outpouring of a compassionate heart
In sync with a brainstorming mind
Guided by an exhorting spirit
To capture the moment
Now or never.

Correctional Born-Again

It never crossed my mind
That I would be born again during detention
Since I was daft and clueless like Nicodemus
Fixated on the impossibility
Of re-entering his mother's womb
Until the idea of the earth's belly sprang to mind
Stilled by silence, bereft of sunshine in the earth's crust
The metamorphic rock is pregnant with treasures,
The costly desideratum of the world
My mind began perceiving unknown brands of gemstones
Concealed within lopes of compressed brains

In the correctional corner

Jail is, indeed, a gold mine
Into which parents hate to see their children descend
But suppose that mining would awaken their minds,
And sharpen their brains
Upgrading them to refine thoughts
Arresting cravings, changing behavior
Turning jeering peers into friends eager to copy their rare art
Imitating Joseph who excelled in manners in a jail uterus
Rewarded with a visa for a glorious exit to Pharaoh's palace
Where he interpreted the Egyptian monarch's dream
Solving a mystery, winning beyond physical freedom

That same Joseph became a young and gifted Prime Minister,
Second only to the king, saving the world from famine,
I too from my cell belly with dimming daylight
Could compose the letters of the alphabet
Set them into motion, casting their shadows on the wall
By pairing, pairing up, and pairing off
Then matching, mixing, and mismatching terms

Juggling diction, raising, and lowering phonology,
Researching etymology, unmasking idioms
Uncovering and aligning meanings with synonyms
Coining phrases to rid America of "f" words
Inventing terms to replace slurs, and curse language
Conjuring diamond dazzling designations to illumine Africa
Banishing mental shackles in a split second
Initiating and proposing therapeutic colloquy
Kissing the sinking cheeks of inmates,
Energizing, mobilizing, and multiplying hugging hands
Warming hearts to flutter in blissful chitchats.

Disappointment Make-Over Lab

My reversion to creeping as if suddenly struck by paralysis
Gnawed away at my bubbly personality
I wallowed in self-pity in the company of crabs and crawlies
I washed my soul with profuse tears flowing like a stream
Hoping they would rescue me from dying the death of fools
Else, what else could I surrender to overcome regret,
Shattering hope at every turn?
Was the question that haunted me endless nights.
With countless sores cropping up in my broken heart

For fear of passing out indefinitely,
I practiced deep breathing on the spot
After slow-motion aerobic exercises
Both to sustain me and to help me delve into my soul
For whom else but myself to encourage me?
Yet, I remained numb, too dumb
To foresee the underlying appointment
Until I made tiny efforts to console myself.
Gradually, my mind yielded to hope
When I began recalling the course of nature
The darkness of night changing into the brightness of day

Inch by inch, the semblance of a renaissance
From the renewing of thought began refreshing my being
Till I began craving fertility in a barren land,
Conjuring an oasis in the desert
So, I proceeded to create room for optimism,
If not, embrace a hell mate as the only other option.
Then I heard Yahweh calling out Lazarus from a frozen grave
A reverberation jump-starting
The mellow whispering of my soul
Inviting me to walk through the narrow gate
And slam negativity

Soon, I began thinking of the nativity,
A star shining over a manger
Ideas flowing in rhythm with my genetic bank
Issuing multifaceted life skill lessons
Then my revived spirit
In drips
Began
Releasing
Healing ointment
Sipping into the very bottom of deep disappointment
Resuscitating a brand new me
Exhuming latent talents
Buried in anguish

Now I am contemplating
What a loss to myself and my community
Had I not been bound awhile!

Criticize Me, I Beg of You

Criticize me, I beg of you, my friend
Prick me softly like the ripe hivea tree
Ready to let its milk ooze out into hanging pots
Otherwise, the children won't have rubber
To protect their feet
If not, with what shall we make wheels for bikes and cars?

Criticize me, but please, don't dismember me
Be careful like my mother digging the earth with her hoe
To till the soil, uprooting weeds without searing the plants
If not, there will be no grains, veggies, and fruits
To nourish millions waiting for the abundance of harvests

Criticize me, I plead, but just between you and I
Not in whispers to others like a sword that stabs in the back
Choose your words, measure them, time them
And warn me in time to go on my knees willfully to listen
So, upon rising, I become finer, taller, smoother
Thanks to the mending words of your redeeming criticism.

Deliver Me

Each waking moment
A trial of trailing nightmares
Struggles signaling paradoxes
Several traps I've fallen into headlong
Hard of hearing, too trusting is the thorn in my flesh
Yet, when I cry out, "why again?"
Begging that you keep Satan away
You insist he is a crucial player on earth's battlefield
His taunting a perfect wake-up call for every salvation soldier
"Cling onto me to redeem the time,
Energy, wealth, and losses," you urge.
So, I am casting my cares onto your everlasting arms
While You turn his lying, stealing, meanness,
And menaces to my advantage
"The risk to catch a cold is perpetual
On polluted planet earth," I complain
"Each morning's refreshing air,
Seasonal winds are enough," You entreat
"Angels on mission rescuing round the clock," You add
Just one more plea I make:
Deliver me from the obsession of deliverance
"Better be obsessed with deliverance
Than fall into the deception
Of once saved, always saved", You caution.

Martyrdom

Waddling to the nowhere destination of self-styled prisoners
Into the inner chamber of acquiescing premature pensioners
Seeking the subterranean lock-up of possessed sojourners
Dead to deadening blows by base men barred from discerners
They waste away in workstations as innocent whinners
Mingling with recruited churchgoers
Serving as fervent feigners
For amoral followership with unprincipled trainers
Unable to resist Christmas-gift-celebrated profaners
Driven into the dreadful pit reserved for shameless scorners
Kneeling at frightening altars with incantation diviners
Chocking with smoking fires
Fueling the fears of trembling petitioners
Facing eerie darkness prolonged to crush unsettling manners
Inhabiting forbidden abysmal depths unknown to abstainers
Impossible to save this generation genuflecting to maligners
With analyzing and conditioning by psycho-physio spinners
Only in renaissance can they shun the toxic dregs of ruiners.

Addiction

I listened to my inmate friend
Intent on grasping the logic of addiction
A tale about desiring
And pleading for one's own death warrant
With survival chances as thin as the edge of a knife's blade
What a reputation for craving
And caving in to an avalanche of unsightly scars!
Sending chills to the family
Like an ice wall hemmed in by a cul-de-sac
The recidivist's drug of choice,
Pungent like wild bitter leaf juice
Numbs the senses
Like a bloody blow, creating attention deficit
Till chilling winter ceases,
Ushering in exuberant summer activities
A change of season,
An opportunity to wrestle free from the curse
Without which,
It lingers like blotches on a dismembered personhood.

A Shoulder on Which to Cry

In the early afternoon,
The deputy brought me some good news
"You have a guest," he announced.
I stood up and followed him
Through the corridor, wondering.
I walked into the hall and he pointed to a cubicle.
"Oh, brother, sister!" I shouted, and that was all.
I couldn't hug them because of the iron gulf between us
But something else was choking me
Impossible for them to understand, much less help

The sack of emotional pain piling up since I was condemned
On top of the stress from a four-hour drive from my locale
Compounded by the quintupled weight
Of handcuffed arms, alone!
All stuck in my throat for unending hours
Over days and nights
While I struggled to come to grips
With my predicament
Like mother hen caught in a trap
On a rescue mission of her chicks
Unconsciously, uncontrollably,
It instantly burst open in front of them
As if a new blade had touched some worn-out fabric

Exhausted for driving for about ten long hours
My brother and sister-in-law defied the shatter of fatigue
Doing their utmost best to stop me from falling apart
Instead, their consolation unleased an avalanche
From a bleeding heart
Drenching my inmate outfit to dripping wet
Their tender words
Of repeated "*ashia**, *ashia ya**" were injections

Piercing the skin of my inner being right through my veins
On the spot my interminable river of hot tears gushed out
Causing my brother to let go
Of his machismo, and crying along

When the time was out, I returned to my cell
Where I pondered over the impact of a face-to-face meeting
Neither their previous telephone calls
Nor that of my girlfriend
Had provoked such overwhelming emotions
Conversations which had really whipped up my spirit

But while facing them, instead of rejoicing
I sobbed uncontrollably
Like an abandoned baby
Upon seeing its approaching mother
Expressing the intensity of undue distress
Or was it that their beholding of my demeaning apparel
Had confirmed the denuding of my essence
Like the undoing of my persona?

Ashia is Pidgin English for "I am sorry" or "Take heart"
Ya is usually added for emphasis.

Sitting on The Fence

Confused by booze, misled by weed
They reject solid ground, preferring the swaying fence
In readiness to fabricate clones of soulless identity
At the cyber altar of ubiquitous laissez-faire,
In the name of liberty
To legate to generations of fast cash grabbers
The hollowness of modern arrogance labeled "western"

Behold the superficiality of individualism of Lucifer incarnate
Encrusting personhood deformities
Into a submission to interminable mental battles
Lacking a sense of direction
Due to fashionable artificial parenting
Blurring the choice
Between heaven's principles and hell's hubris
Preferring the wretchedness of lukewarmness

How shall they stand in the judgment,
Having undermined their celestial identities
Refusing to seize the thresholds
Paving the tracks of each condemnation
Boastfully turning down the lifetime opportunity to choose
Wisely and humbly, energy over lethargy?

Clinging onto the fence, seeking celebrity status
In Nowhere nation
Faintly appearing on the fictional map of comedy playwrights
Featuring projections of Buffoon Avenue where fools flock
To wallow in their perpetual lack of personality
The aggravated perpetuation of meanness
Until eventual banishment into eternal oblivion.

Survival Ship

Where do I stand among economic victims exiled in droves?
Trapped on survival ships, jam-packed,
Crossing troubled waters
After swimming through the abyss
Of treacherous ocean depths
Where energetic and devouring sharks
And whales are stewards
To the wonderland of flaunted wealth
Seeking the fittest in the rat race.
Dropping their innate talents and circumstantial cargos
To settle for crumbs
Falling off the tables of moguls on Lady Liberty island

Is my lock-up comparable to jolting canoes
Carrying countless passengers?
Hundreds of times beyond capacity,
Courting capsizing at every wave?
I lack the skill of a deep-sea diver,
Exploring the bottom without sinking
I will venture only to serve myself whole
On the kitchen platter of the ocean
Where excited sharks and sea lions
Will grab my head for dinner
Before my fighting hands reach the shore
For crumbs for breakfast

Should I whine in the safety of my cell
Overlooking frightened immigrants?
Plunging into roaring waves head-on without swimming gear
Yet, for compassion sake, survivors,
Hitherto unknown in their fatherland,
Will stand a better chance
To display uncultivated talents, and shine

Having escaped the tortuous set-ups
Of innumerable bottlenecks
Willfully inserted at every stage
Of growth in their land of birth

Refugees with a track record of surviving by hook or by crook
Toil round the clock
To catch a glimpse of feasting *à l'américaine*
As if in a replay of Noah's ark beckoning for eternal survival
Willing to earn some fast cash, sacrificing self and dignity
For the value of tips, piles of cents of the alluring dollar
While managers feed fat on their sweat in plush getaways.

Bypassing God

Am I in chains because I refused to bypass God?
Is it possible to bypass God and win a pass to the top?
I will pass out if my arrest isn't indeed a narrow,
Winding mountain pass

If I am foolhardy to bypass God,
From whose subsoil do I dig out life treasures?
By whose wisdom do I know the difference
Between good and evil?
By whose foreknowledge do I brace up for tragedies?
By the light of whose prophecy do I perceive beyond sight?
By whose guidance
Am I heading towards the Promised Land?
By whose design and molding am I looking so resplendent?
By whose omnipotence have I been protected since birth?

Bypassing God is tantamount to presuming
That good luck is plucked by the ticking of a clock
Bypassing God, a game we used to play,
Relying solely on our brains to pass.
When unbeknown to us
Failure with men could mean passing with God.

Mistake

I missed the irrevocable take
Picking poison in place of panacea
For a split second, the vulnerability of my humanity laid bare
Dizzy, waning, and limping on Jericho Road Sanitorium
An angel with lightning speed came to my rescue
Armed with a leaf from the tree of twelve fruits
For the healing of fallen nations, nursing damaged nerves
Reversing the tragic consequences of my mistake
Thanks to grace, humans do not die from erring
But erring without recess
Does bear the inevitable consequence
Of audaciousness that outsmarts the late persons,
The penalty for their presumptuousness
Now too late to be sorry in their breathless state.

From Facial to Soul Make-Up

Drops of water in sprays of fragrance
Strokes of powder on layers of cotton
Dozens of pencils, brushing over coloration
Human construction smearing divine constitution
Fruit of science labs impersonating vanity,
Coverup for virgin beauty
Currently in composition
In a million studios dotted in global parlors
A hundred hand-propelled circles lifting jaws, poking cheeks

Cleansing, brushing, rubbing, polishing
Unmaking, coating, refreshing, wiping
Mounting and moving in cycles round the clock
Constant and compelling in rhythm with breathing
All for the pride of self to feed the lust of the eyes.
Daily modes of facial perfection keeping pace
To celebrate its glory in the world of city dorms

Where are you, facial foundation, in this bottom belly?
Which eyes shall admire your stunning attractiveness?
Which artist can refute the temporality
Of synthetic beauty at hell's gate?
Who pines for facelifts
When dedication to soul-searing is urgent?
Why splurge on looks in vogue
Without the mirrors of admiring eyes to behold?

Shouldn't my Maker orthograph
My idiosyncratic features now?
Repairing the tarnishes of my character
Without the obstruction of self?
Shouldn't the Creator's original design
Be visible in heaven's hall of fame?

Angels awed at my enduring beauty despite the fall
Before I quit this amoebic encasement?

Cheering Angel

My confinement
Is the retreat of an aging eagle
Else, how can I transcend self
Without this vital rebirth?
A scalpel from heaven
Operating with surgical precision
Making a wholesome change
While I persevere with endurance
Willingly banishing loquaciousness
Embracing prolonged silence
Tapping wisdom from listening
So sobering the spirit reigns
In a bare-bone existence
Under enforced anonymity
Focusing on necessities
Waiting on a timely design
While nature takes its course
Growing brand new wings
Equipped to fly to higher skies
Towering above my expectations
Moving my guardian angel to cheer
And pausing to whisper repeatedly,
"Can opaque darkness eclipse a star?"

Metamorphosis

They imposed a limitation on my movements–
I declared a sabbatical
From purposeless time-consuming outings.
They eclipsed sunshine–
Behold the mandatory illuminating of my thoughts!
They drastically reduced my speech–
I perfected my listening skills with the small inner voice.
They obstructed my distant parenting–
I thanked God for fostering care
From kin and compassionate connections.
They arrested social networking–
I used the least chance to make friends with my jail mates.
They denied me daily personal care–
Welcome to a retreat to gear myself up for future adversities.
They interrupted access to my workstation–
Who can erase my signature
On everyone and things I have touched?
They served insipid meals–
I conjured up salt at dinner table
Especially when I am starving.
They halted my projects and hobbies–
I brainstormed daily on how to compensate for the loss.
They turned my life into a disgrace–
Minute by minute I upheld my intrinsic worth.
They belittled me with strict orders–
I made up my mind to take each one respectfully.
They treated me like a criminal–
Yet my conscience was clear.
In a sense I was a prisoner of conscience.

PART 3

LIFE IN JAIL

Monotony

Stripped of the rejuvenation of my vivacious personality
Downgraded to wearing hand-me-down uniforms
Detoured from the avenues of my diversified activities
Redirected onto the guarded passage of constricted corridors
Deprived of the savoring
Of ginger biscuits and hot pepper soup
Served basic cheese, canned veggies,
And dollar cookies on the go
Resigned to the sameness of days without novel expectations
Refused the glow and warmth of healing sunlight
Let loose at night like a rat to embrace in toto
The dullness of routine without perks.

Boot Camp

This place must be boot camp, hell for numskulls
The site for enforced mental oxygenation
To delete engraved falsehood that deforms manhood
Not a season during which to swoon or snooze
For booze is the last thing you'd ever screw
Much less a phenomenal weed to sniff or chew
Through the impassable lane of psychological makeover
In the martial maternity of mental labor
To rebirth deluded youth, to chart a new course

Frequent ultimatums steer muscle-flexing exercises
Hand-cuffed, heart-chained to enforce creeping and crawling
Vaporizing hot pepper facials
For sneezing and coughing up toxins
Chasing away the mischief of peers and indoctrinators
Replaying and back-masking to up-root traces of tainting,
Dissuading from anti-social simulated robotic stunts
To rescue from drowning brains in devilish dummy droning

Boot camp is a demeaning baptismal lock-up
Between hard concrete and barbed walls impossible to scale
Repeated disciplining banning naughtiness until submission
Banging the rod of correction scouring rusted misdeeds
To banish cursing learned from the faculty of trash talk

Boot camp is a school for rules without exception
Where shouted commands
Test the mettle to provoke yielding
No chances to indulge body cravings rocking the brain
While the iota and grip
Of recited mantras are resetting the psyche
With grilling instructions, reforming until the final resolve
To take the narrow way upon graduation from boot camp.

Chow Time

"It's chow time, ladies,"
For what is a better name for jail grub?
"Common, let's go,"
The Deputy's voice rings through the living room
Into the twenty cells of Gulf East

Touc, touc, touc, twenty times
On each door of the private cells
Unlocking automatically to remote control off-location
In a successive order of military correctness
In the prison housing area
Of Erie County in Buffalo, New York

Lunch is a hotdog, peanut butter,
Or salami with slices of white bread
A drink of milk gulped down amidst nibbles of salad
Treat chicken and potato or pizza by the cut

"Last time for chow," the voice thunders away at dawn
The eerie sound, catching up with early morning sleep-in
Is indeed the final call for wartime breakfast *à l'Américaine*
All hail to cereal, milk, juice, and fruit
Usher in Kellogg bigtime, and Mills at times
A quick transfer of each serving
From the thick plastic aging white, maroon trays
Into the bright orange tee-shirt of each inmate
Turned into a basket of chow harvest
For whom indeed can gulp it all down cold
In less than five minutes between five and six a.m.
Upon jumping out of a deeply troubled slumber
Another winter morning in prison?

Pining for A Special Guest

Barred from the garden,
I can't admire you, cute floating butterfly
Much less, out of the essential shrub,
You are rare, fluttering ladybird
With my door sealed and space so clean,
You are barred, nasty cockroach
I dare you to fly thousands of miles
To suck out my blood, biting mosquito
Who would tell me the hour of the night
Without you, crowing cock?
Isn't it great there's no marsh around for you, croaking toad?
I'm having fun smirking at you
From my soilless base, gliding worm
Aren't you smart enough to slip in
Through the ceiling, shy wall gecko?

Above all else, Miss ant, you are designed to sneak in and out
Reaching homes, rich and poor in search of crumbs
Plus, in the absence of rain,
You can safely slip in under my door
So, why don't you sneak out of the lawn, traverse the stairs
Stealthily make your way
By the edges of the concrete and come on?
I have something super for you; it's all yours for the taking

Guess what? A grain of rice fell off my plate today
And Mumtaz swore that it had not been destined for me
So, I saved it in the palm of my hands for you
See, it's under the door, inviting you to my still, friendly space
It is a long-grain,
Two soldiers can carry it safely back to the nest
To feed the colony, energize the soldiers
To finish the new anthill

Come on, anty!
I promise
I will not smash you
Instead, I swear on my honor
To bring more grains from the next meal
Let's keep the soldiers working
Miss ant, are you hearing me?
Come on quickly
The queen is waiting
To crown you
For your ingenuity
Especially because of…,
guess what?
Your finesse
Despite
Your
Tininess.

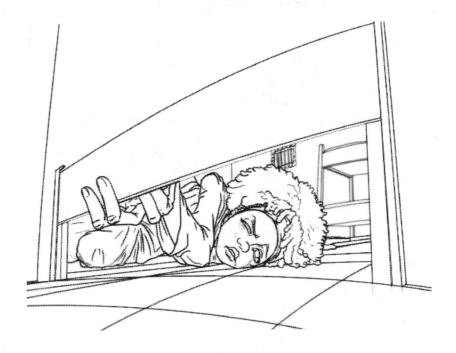

Listen

Listen to the soft sound of silence
The reality of seeming nothingness
Quick movements obliging a deep breath,
Gasping, catching, holding, letting out, oof!
The inhaling and exhaling of air, fresh and stale
In rhythmic succession of input and output
While a magnificent sight takes away breath
Compelling a pause to catch one's breath
Quintessence of existence
Quickening the vitality of spontaneity
Organs pumping, transporting, transmitting
Informing, reforming, signaling, moving one to action

Listen to the flushing foams of the ocean and rivers
Gushing waves washing, touching,
Rubbing, deforming, forming
Healing breeze brushing, hushing,
Whispering, refreshing, caressing

Listen to the pain, her version of your accusation
Contradicting in flip side your trashing conviction
Crushing your urge to rush in condemnation

Listen to the dashing away of crawlies
The swashing of sneaky trotters
Tweeting birds in bending branches
Clapping leaves of waving trees lifting your spirits

Listen to the exhorting reason from your conquering mind
Blending with the acquiescing beating of your contrite heart
And the resounding warning from your guiding conscience
Knocking, pleading, appealing, repeating, insisting
Shiii, shiii, shiii, listen.

Catching My Breath

Here's evidence I was born at the dying minute
In my generation
I am a workaholic, schooling for life,
Aching with stress, multitasking is my middle name
Mothering young and old babies round the clock
Lost on cyber, going snail pace in an age of rapid technology
Slaving on do-it-yourself jobs in a touch-button age

Weary of replicating my great grandma
Nibbling on leisure and pleasure
Repeatedly trapped between sunset and sunrise
Pushing back premature wrinkles in my youth
Flexing muscles to keep pace with passing time
Scrunching for money, running after flying time,

Desperate for wisdom to adjust to my time of life in real time
I long for an opportunity to catch my breath and save time
Like Samson wiping out Philistines, at last,
Making up for wasted time
Or Ruth losing time in exile, returning
For the climax of her life in time
Or Esther risking her life to confront Haman
Before execution time
Or a tree shedding its leaves in winter
To revive in spring in time
Hoping and expecting my extra and late shifts,
Spread over time,
Would lead to the extending of my hibernation time
For now, I'm hurrying to graduate with honors in time
Without having to catch my breath,
Energized to have a great time.

The Oven Zone of Hell

Upon return from the airport, sighing in chagrin
Marking forty interminable days of shut-in anguish
My flight canceled, the snow was faulted
I was ordered out of my quiet familiar space
To the noisy zone of mocking frightened fellows
Howling from the depths of the quaking dungeon
Muffling my pressing petition for revival

Desperate for sleep within earshot of deafening cells
Occupants banging walls in a continual cacophony
Venting daytime misery and rehearsing nightmares
My flagging spirit kept sinking, O! for how long?
My boggled mind caused my pounding heart to race,
O! for how long?
Maniacal outbursts within the haunted zone,
O! for how long?
I implored my guardian angel to keep me intact,
While it lasted
O! for how long?

A Plea for Life Sentencing

Modern Lifestyle, ML for short, is guilty
Of estrangement and abandonment
Of children in the crib, parents on the run
Else, how did youth of knowledgeable parents
As well as those from wealthy homes
Land in jail?
How did their flight crash onto ground zero?

Whether you are Mr., Mrs, or Miss Modern Lifestyle,
The charges against you fill ledger pages:

Dysfunctional parenting
Abuse and taunting by loved ones
Broken hearts chasing after the umpteenth divorce case
Loneliness resulting in indulgence in forbidden videos
Compulsive munching of addictive,
Modified, refined crunches
The popping of mood-altering supplements
More couch potatoes
Viewing a chain of series round the clock

Interminable telephone calls
Succumbing to the tyranny of peers driven by trends
Paging, cellular phone and internet day and night
Deviant TV talk shows on the increase
Brain-munching computer games
Entertaining, nightclubbing, rapping, boozing
Powder room infectious talks on pornography

Doing day-time jobs, taking night-time classes
Employers' Mammon-driven agendas
Round the clock gambling
Welfare scrounging for life-depleting pleasures

Annual traditions outspending credit cards
Bowing to multiple social pressures
Falling for mystical seductions

For committing the above crimes in the name
Of Civilization
Of modernity
Of industrialization
Of development

Mr., Mrs, Miss Modern Lifestyle
Or whatever you call yourself,
You are sentenced without appeal
To life,
Lasting the lifetime of humanity on earth!

PART 4

BUILDING RESILIENCE

Grace

Grace for me on reserve
Something I did not deserve
According to the flouted divine law
That brought me laying so low

Grace, for me, accorded again
At the time of mounting pain
As it must be so for an oyster
A pearl beyond logic for nature to foster

For who could imagine a wholesome birth
Being the product of a troublesome death
When gain was gone, enemies jeering
Behold the dawn of mirthful cheering.

Jewels in Jeopardy

Behold priceless jewels shut in behind sturdy steel bars
Dabbling in the boredom of indefinite lockdown
Suddenly, the sealed doors fling open like lions' dens
They rush out to reminisce about diverse missed pleasures
What a sparkle in the eyes of hitherto listless inmates!

Momentarily, they stand blameless,
Disregarding their Achilles' heels
Sharing dreams of wonders imagined and projected
Emanating from the essence
Of their perfectly created ancestors
A glimpse of Eden before the ouster of Adam and Eve
A split second when their past acts of daring rebellion
Go into oblivion like turned-over smeared pages of their lives
Anecdotes pouring out from chatting lips,
Exposing white teeth
Shinning like diamonds in-between layers
Of the dark depths of the earth
Scintillating conversations in tune
With the caged birds of Maya Angelou

Free like swinging branches in a caressing breeze,
They conjure up images of the rays
Of the craved and missed sunshine
Now couched in twinkling stars decorating the sky
Lavishing their beauty in arrays of glowing colors
Voraciously, they struggle to recapture the smears
Flickering from the dangling constellation
In the brightness flanked by the darkness of night
They dare to bare their souls beside guards in surveillance
The laughter of inmates is like the sun caressing unsightliness

Though condemned for crimes as varied as their faces

Happily, they embrace each other like innocent children
Reigniting an aura of warmth causing their hearts to flutter
What relief for someone to acknowledge your worth!
On friendly shoulders, they lean, moan, weep, and hope
In self-acceptance, facing the truth, they stand tall
Like leafless trees in winter towering amid frozen weeds
With the weight of their sentence
Rendering grace more recherché
Like Prince Charming rescuing Cinderella
From black cellar cinders

Night after night, they indulge in the recess of mutual respect
Coping gracefully with disfigurements
Caused by irresistible cravings
Like fallen angels, they seize the fleeting, treasured minutes
Freely sharing ideas, opinions, and feelings,
Consoling each other
An ensemble of mixed cultures,
Reflecting snapshots of resplendence on their faces
Unnoticed, misplaced, and neglected jewels,
Awaiting rescue from jeopardy.

Confession

The sin that springs to mind is lying
Not the vicious type like bearing false witness
Since elementary school, I have never lied to obtain passes
Neither have I ever plagiarized to get good grades
Nor did I ever sell groundnuts in a punched measuring cup
I am not the type to lie about my feelings,
Especially towards a guy

The kind of lying that I am lisping about is lightweight
Whose effect cannot be compared to the hard blow
Of a heavy-weight boxer in the ring

Indeed, my lies are like gentle caresses
Preventing shocks as well as the disappointment
Of mates and all
What a constraint from hurting other people's feelings!
Concurrently, they prop up a good image of myself
Thanks to them, I maintain relationships with my partners
They are as protective as a shawl,
Handy in the changing weather
Or as image-preserving as a wig on bald hair

They are merely snippets of misinformation flying in the air,
Coming in timely for use with good intentions
Besides, I am not the only one who is guilty
Of decorating truth with them
Pseudo-intellectuals and rappers flash them past naked truths

But recently, I perceived a treacherous contortion of my lips
Because, instead of one, they arrived in a horde
Instead of taking a direct route, they orbited before landing
Each dangling in my face prompting me to choose them
Thus, I have caught myself lately telling lies by reflex

Like coughing, they dash out of my lips without permission

The truth is, I have always restricted my cherished pack of lies
To calculated use, with sputtering allowed,
And dismissal forthwith
But right now, they are like free radicals
Lingering like flaking lipstick
Worst of all, I am beginning to eat my words,
Stammering all along
Or have I inhaled them, lodging them in my subconscious?
If not, why do I often say, "well"
When I am feeling like "hell"?
Why do I nod in agreement when indeed I am clueless?
Why do I take an appointment
When it is certain that I can't honor it?
Why do I say that I am just a few steps away
When I am miles off?
Why do I accuse traffic jams of my late arrival
When there is none?
Why do I blame the lack of parking space
When I get to a meeting late?

Spotlessly white and harmlessly trivial— furtively, lies appear
Unable to bruise or cause a frown— promptly, lies endear
An army of invading Lilliputians— each armed with a spear
As small as ants, nothing to compare with caterpillars—
A phony will swear
Spewing out as from a vending machine—
A fabricator's exposed lie to clear
Startled by a partner's unexpected follow-up questions—
They disappear
Zi Zi Zi, on a chronic liar's shaking lips as if with mud—
They resurface to smear

What's more eerie is the aftermath of lying
After firing one like a missile to shatter truth

Shame covers me all over like a wet blanket
My eyes go blinking as if there is dirt in them
I can barely shoot a glance at my party
Then a haunting question steals my appetite
Am I not shooting myself in the leg?
Anxiety takes over, causing me to worry
What if he or she finds out the truth?

All through the night I can't stop grieving,
I keep asking myself why, how,
And for what ultimate purpose?
Deep down in my gut,
I feel my intestines twitching and twisting
I stand in front of the mirror
And all I see are tatters of shattered truth
Instead of a steady glow on my face,
I perceive goose bumps of blatant lies
It is obvious that I am becoming
An old haggard shadow of myself
Have I sold my soul so cheaply to the devil?
What if the Ananias-Sapphira syndrome strikes me?
What if vicious lies begin streaming into my brain?
Who on earth will ever trust me?
O, Lord, have mercy!
Reset my conscience.
Rid me of lies, chronic or occasional.

A Box-full of Confessions

I am sorry for the waste of immeasurable time and energy,
Riding on the Commonway highway of charming choices,
Failing to follow the Narrowway pathway of good faith
For which I almost became as wretched as a scarecrow

I am sorry for denying my subordinates a fair hearing
Mistakenly equating excellent credentials
To a mark of character
Thus, I cheated myself
By undermining their complementary qualities
For, what good is a brilliant mind in a heart of stone?

I do admit that I have been dressing for vanity
I should have been more honest
By confessing my lack of self-esteem
Accepting myself is humility that plucks up a lot of courage
For, high quality in modesty is more empowering

I regret yielding to workaholism so often at my job
Yet, whenever I have paused to appreciate my achievements,
Taken a rest to eat and get some fresh air,
In the end, I accomplish more than I had programmed

I denounce the recurrent urge to compromise principle
It is indeed clear evidence of lack of self-control
I need to decide in advance
And keep practicing the good example
By so doing, I will motivate others to respect the law

Sometimes, I bend over backwards to please others
But in hindsight I groan,
Recalling how some beneficiaries slighted me
Yet those who truly merit praise never require or expect it

For there is a stark difference between lookalikes
Between a radiant and a forced smile
Between silence and mere lip service
Between assertiveness and obsequiousness
Between the front door that opens to new ideas
And the back door that clouds judgment, hindering progress
Between fulfilling the requirements and gaining favor

Did you notice
That I have not even mentioned the sins of omission?
And do you think that my list of confessions is exhaustive?

Character

Character is a garden within the forest of life
A daily eking, and not the job of a fast farthing
Even if you compute the wages due to the earth
After ingesting the seed, and feeding the world
The soil, weather, seeds, are none of your makings
Weeding, mulching, and pruning
Is mere evidence of your mettle
How others judge you and your role,
Is a marketplace you can't avoid
Though tempests, winds, lightning,
And thunder you cannot tame
Yet, the greater the storms of life,
The better you weather them
As the mark of the gradual molding of more sterling qualities
Character, so indelible; it lives on after you have passed on.

Invisible Gift

It is more costly than diamond
You consider it more superior than your worth
For it is as bright as the sun
That scares the darkness in you
It is bigger than the ocean
Just how can you contain it?
As tall as the sky
Who are you to aim so high? you shriek
It's prettier than a rose, tenderness its backbone
You dare not imagine you deserve it
It brings balance, order, and resets priorities
Putting a break to your ongoing dissonance
It seeks your attention, yet escapes your notice
Sadly, you are yet too busy existing than living
Its patience is divine, what a quiet still voice!
Only with discernment can you behold the invisible gift
Grab it and show your desire to die for it
For, none but you, by tasting it, can esteem it
To the point of sacrificing all for it
Its application is the only way
To establish beyond counsel
Your purpose in life

Name it and seize it!

Yes or No

The ongoing tug of war
Perpetually pitting reason against sentiments
Step by step and breath after breath during a lifetime
In matters affecting the destiny of the soul
Only one must stand out to shut in the other
Like a swinging door

Yes may seem right from the start
Silencing No may look quite smart
But time and wisdom reveal which is right
Like virtue and vice, quite distinct in destiny's design
Set far apart as an ocean boundary between land masses
The contrast is parallel to day deleting night
Unfailingly in time
Analogous to blessings banning curses
From a celestial heritage
Roses arising intact in-between thorns as in nature
Prosperity pouncing on poverty with a touch of compassion

Yes and No are two life companions, inseparable
Inevitably staring at opposite directions
Like two sides of a fabric
Antonyms, adversaries, with each one claiming the stage
Yet, it is forever resolved
That only one can be showcased at a time

Easy on the surface is the Yes of a roaring crowd
But tough within the pith
Is the definitive No of the one who stands alone
Yea and Nay are brothers in a timeless tussle at the core
Within the element of being with self-evident outcomes
Products of the weighing and the making of choices
In the end, displaying a roadmap

Of No's conviction
Side by side
Yes' persuasion
The choice is yours
Between Yes and No.

Walk on Water

As a graduate of jail-time Handy Man College
You would not regret missing lectures in amphitheaters
With better tools at the shop, validate your prison cell toil
A perfected skill commands diplomas short of experience
Offer first-rate service, realizing beyond your dreams
Pursue your mission, excel without primetime publicity
Your accomplishments in the hood will cruise continents
Promptly, you will sell your time-tested edition
To competing Metropolitan dealers
Proud of their redeemed youth

Learn to cook like a chef with rare recipes,
Specializing in ambrosia
Sing from the pith of pain and penitence,
For birds will hush to listen
Adopt the gait of self-confidence,
Children will rush into your arms
After a demo of your art,
Youngsters will hail you as their model
If you apply for the unique position,
Employers will grab you fast
When you analyze a situation,
Your boss will hang up his phone
When you interact with fellows, neighbors behold a genius

While you walk on water, empty yourself of self
Beware of Peter's self-consciousness
That plunged him into the lake, near drowning, but for Jesus
Neither go to sleep like Buddha enjoying his nirvana
Focus on your clients, registering their diverse wishes
Daily striving to adjust to changing needs
Till you reach the apogee of your unique design
Warranting admiration without sponsored promotion.

PART 5

HINDSIGHT AND FORESIGHT

My Life Is Game

My life's been a bumpy ride
Weathering storms, thunders and tempests
Bruises and scars my evidence
Challenges lingering, tougher with age and year
For as long as I've known myself in consciousness
From weaning from mother's loins at too tender an age
To withstand daily toils in life's battles
Like confronting daggers drawn in and out of the battlefield

I've gone the extra mile, consoling the wounded on my way
From peers at school to friends in the hood
At ten, I was placed at the catering frontline
Vis-à-vis vibrant women of twenties and thirties
To face tasks designed for womanhood and motherhood
At home like outside, I was caught up in fights
Atypical of my generation
Though staying out of trouble and gossips about conflicts

Now I'm in my forties and maimed in a sudden battle
My heart's bleeding, my mind taunted
While peers are wondering in shock and shuddering
At my venturing alongside the grown and the seasoned
Clueless that I had no say on assignment types and numbers
On the stage of life on which circumstances catapulted me
Like trekking on a long trail coping with hunger pangs

Indignant, I look back, yet grateful for escaping bombs
Though thunder rumbled through my abode at recess
When the dragon targeted my home unawares
Provoking brawls resulting from wanton villainy
At the very peak of family harmony
Flinging my sons and daughters into the wilderness
While landing me within prison gates

Unfairly attacked by unknown enemies without signals
While I wasn't even guilty, neither my offspring
Of hating our neighbors or envying the rich
Let alone boasting of our abundance
I had no choice but to step into the arena naked,
Without an armor, shield, nor breastplate
In self-defense in the heat of warfare

Reckoning this numbing blow
Must be the ultimate onslaught
Surviving which, I will forever put on
The whole armor of omnipotence
Round the clock in vigilance
Bracing up for battles declared or abrupt
Dreaded and daunting.

Devotion to Deception

You, my traveling companion, you promised pain with gain
To which I agreed and signed up on the spot
As you handed me the gear for the sport
Pledging your endearing presence each step of the way

The road ahead was layered in stretches of variegated terrain
Slippery, thorny, treacherous, winding along precipices
Sudden bends with cracks and crevices
Throwing me off-balance
On and off-season by foot,
Toes caught between rocks and hard places

I've been on the trail beyond a decade
Feeling, bearing the pain, piling up with increasing yawns
I yearn for the sharing of the gain
So much I begin to wonder if it's all a game

Here and now, I demand the fulfillment of your vow
Having analyzed the very nature of the equation:
Your multiple and unexplained absences
Spent in picturesque cottages
Can't balance the years, the blisters on my toes,
And unquenched thirst
Add undue silence and sighs
Replacing your spontaneous smiles
Plus, your abrupt and premature halts
Signaling a breach of trust

So, must I, my household, and dependents keep trekking
On slippery roads with several forks without a map?
Must I obey your current order
To go on holding on as if waiting for Godot?
When is the end of forever hoping

To benefit from undeclared stacks of gain?
While you go on naming and changing destinations
Only found in space?

Having seized my staff and gone ahead without looking back
Are you different from a chameleon,
A dupe, a con artist à la feymania?
Inebriated by a concoction of tales, lies, follies,
Which, like strong wine
You have drunk yourself into a stupor
Midway into your uncharted highway
Having reneged on your promise,
Buttressed by fabrications and forgeries
A boomerang, like a tornado,
Is shattering your bogus personality
The mirage you chase while intoxicated
By ill-gotten gain from my pain
Which you have consciously caused "*sans souci*"*
Because of your lifelong devotion to deception.

Sans souci: French for "without any worry"

Save the Planet

The wellbeing of the planet was at stake
After a sudden attack by aliens
They were giants escorted by unidentified flying boats
Quickly, they gratified the first residents they encountered
Who soon began serving them as sycophants
Releasing key security secrets of the territory
Turning citizens over to usurpers
In the throes of neocolonialism

To capture the stubborn,
Payola rushed out with fancy packages
Courting people to join the bandwagon of proselytizers
They mainly targeted two security guards at the port of entry
Tool smiled broadly and hugged the revelers
Laughing, giggling, and chanting loudly
While Stone bombarded Payola
With "why" and "what" questions
The invading militia screamed at Stone, threatening arrest
Seeing the danger, Stone rolled away and disappeared
The story of amenable Tool versus resolute Stone went on

Tool kept eyeing the trappings
Of the clout of the control freaks
Bowed to them, then hurried,
And took up residence in plush hotels
With frivolous frolicking waiters offering tipsily nectars
Dining and feasting from city to city, jeering at Stone
It was the beginning of a lifestyle
Of looking out for payoffs to grab
By okey-dokey, Tool gradually drowned his identity
In the pampering illusion of adulation

With integrity, Stone escaped basking

In Apollo's fascinating fire
Dumping favoritism in a corrupting system
Fraught with intemperance
Evicted from his duty post, he embraced self-confidence,
Seizing the chance to track the homesteads of his ancestors
Retreating into the treasure trove of past generations
Uncovering values linking to the present,
Projecting into the future
Finally, he drew a secure roadmap with precision and caution

One day the clock turned around,
Signaling the changing season
The world watched in wonder the fall of oppressors
Tyrants ceding to the day of reckoning
With groans and regrets
For prohibiting subjects
From exercising freewill and using their talents

Tool ended up crippled, exhausted, and embittered
Wasted, weak, and vulnerable like a used tire
Facing the nemesis of rashness
Plunging him into a freezing zone

Stone, having toiled and excelled through purposeful pursuits
Was earning interest on his perseverance
Having groomed self, was poised to take charge
While watching Tool pining
In the pangs of death in slow motion

Too late to make up for the loss
Unable to wind back the clock
Tool became poor and beggarly,
Wallowing in despair in city slums
Usher in fireworks for Stone's inaugural.

Skunky Pitcher Reminisces

Upon landing, the sky was blue; the clouds rolled back
I saw the expansive landscape, rivers meandering in blue
Houses rising in-between lofty trees,
Blooming flowers in multicolor

During my ride through the city, the cool breeze kissed me
Trees clapped and chirping birds welcomed me
My tent was ready, couched with the fragrance
Of lavender in the yard

Overnight, I mastered the map and traced my bearings
During each outing,
I found my way around the cardinal points
Friends began calling me up to plan their trips
"But I just got here," I'll say, trying to shy away
"Yes, but you are doing a good job," they would retort.
Everyone I met smiled, everything I touched thrived

Not until I pitched a second tent in the realm of skunks
During this phase of the expedition, the tornado signaling
My deliverance from the harsh weather was an urgent need
The change of coordinates
To chart my future placement pressed on
Grace was over; I became desperate for a new lease on life

I couldn't wait to soar back to my hometown
To retrieve the unique endowments of motherland,
Too often degraded out of greed, for enormous interests
By marauding invaders smirking at hospitable villagers
Yet enforcing laws to outlaw brands
Showcasing the grains of my clan

Despite the roaring of felling timber
Rumbling through destroyed habitations
Exposing the nudity of the raped earth
Amid disappearing rivers
Blinded folks are still desperately yearning for skunk paradise
Fighting, even falsifying files,
Vying for a lifestyle of adulteration
Begging and kneeling for visas
Ensnaring them into consumerism
O, how they keep queuing up at the door of no-return!
For self-sacrificing, modern-day, human resource,
Gorée-boat departures
Millions willfully matching headlong
Into Mammon dictatorship
A rollicking, alluring zone, spotted with skunk settlements.

Lifetime Contest on Planet Human

Virtue is good and vice is evil, and no one disputes that
But does virtue always overcome vice on Planet Human?
Is popular acclaim for mesmerizing performances
The trouncing of virtue?
Only if it wasn't possible for the green lawn
To conceal camouflaging chameleons and the sly snake
Targeting the simple and deceiving the trusting

Intrinsic quality is quintessential, and no one disputes that
But does it always earn extrinsic rewards?
Is the exponential increase of superficial glitters
Not the victory of cheap?
Only if it wasn't possible
For dulled minds and insatiable desires
To lust after fascinating looks and deception
In high and holy places
Where fashion moguls invite tricksters
To flaunt designs in vogue.

Modesty is a high moral prescription,
And no one disputes that
But does it always beat the outrightly indecent?
Is he or she with revealing, attention-getting wear
Not more desirable?
Only if it wasn't possible to sacrifice health and comfort
At the altar of fashion and sex appeal
Bare-footed men and women tread on thorns and thistles
To win a title

Seeking the truth sets free indeed, and no one disputes that
But does the truth always set people free on Planet Human?
Is a tall tale, spiced, baked, and served piping hot
Not more preferred?

Only if it wasn't possible to either make errors
Or to benefit from a lie
Damaging lies have turned some honest people
Into hermits in the wild forest
Where birds sing on purpose, void of flattery or favoritism

The natural look is the authentic one,
And no one disputes that
But is natural always more desirable
Than the synthetic on Planet Human?
Which star would not reinvent himself or herself
To impress the jury?
Only if it wasn't possible
To feign African lips and butt, fair skin,
Long straight Caucasian hair, and Asian glazing makeup.
Modern science and technology
Fabricate twinkles and prostheses
For all intents and purposes,
They create needs beyond imagination

Public personalities should be honest,
And no one disputes that
But is honesty always the best option for the common good?
Are diplomacy, tactfulness, avoidance, and manipulation
Reigning supreme on the mass media?
Only if it wasn't possible to deceive the credulous
And numb the senses
For a fleeting moment, the powerful exploit a tricky situation
In ways acceptable,
To the extent of provoking thunderous applause

Humans are the most intelligent beings,
And no one disputes that
But do they always use their brains for their own benefit?
Don't the unsuspecting millions
Willfully give their votes to demagogues?

Only if it wasn't possible to mislead the electorate
Through moving slogans
And that is clear proof that humans on Planet Earth
Fall for the enchanting
Instead of using their brains at a time
When reason would have rescued them.

Stripped of Dignity

If my education, career, and livelihood
Depended solely on my begetter, *Akong,
I would never have envied Americans
To the point of taking refuge in their land
Warming up their villages with tropical sunshine,
Planting flowers
And smiling with kind and curious neighbors
While unfriendly folks peep, looking unreasonably frightened
By the presence of a displaced woman in agony
Running the risk of losing the vital connection
With her offspring

Yet every thought of my urgent need to return home
Was fraught with obstacles
Why?

Because the most favored CEO, his highness,
The only one conferred with powers
To validate Akong's worth
As well as to facilitate and develop work for all
To render each person's labor a substantial contribution
To the wealth of the community,
His lordship *Keufere, failed, and woefully so

Imagine Akong singlehandedly
Paving the footpath to the spring in the village
Equipped only with a hoe and a cutlass
Despite all the tractors under Keufere's control
Keufere equally failed to dig rural roads,
Not even farm-to-market roads for the women's harvest

Akong worked overtime to cultivate coffee
To increase supply towards Keufere's export scheme

Yet Keufere gave Akong only two hours' worth for eight a day
Too little even to buy scant grocery or pay school fees
Not worthy of the enslaving, time-consuming crop

Akong and his family fasted for a whole year
To buy electric poles and bring light to the quarter
Yet Keufere, despite the material and manpower under him
Did not electrify the whole village.
Neither did he lower the price of kerosene for bush lamps

Akong, as a roving ambassador of the Fon
Went on several dangerous trips
On foot and by bike to keep the peace between villages
Yet Keufere did not install telecommunication networks
Nor pave roads, much less provide public transport
To access remote posts and public halls
Spotted over long distances between villages and cities

Akong worked three separate jobs from youth to adulthood
Daily rising as early as 4 a.m. to undertake the first task
Yet Keufere did not offer any welfare package to families
To support households for raising obedient children
With a good citizenship spirit and superb skills

Akong sewed clothes free for poor villagers,
He and his wife mediated in conflicts between spouses
They even hosted battered women,
Feeding their children and relatives
Yet Keufere refused to establish shelters
For abused women, neither in the village nor in town

Akong did the extraordinary, teaching himself the ABCs
And eventually learning how to read and write
Yet Keufere issued an official school curriculum
That was irrelevant to the occupation of parents
Automatically distancing pupils and students

From their families
The absence of technical training institutions says it all
Thus, men and women went on toiling with stone tools

Akong was a member of the local traditional council
That effectively judged cases in the village
In a timely and effective manner
While promoting the respect of law and order
Yet Keufere ordered the dismantling of that unit

If people everywhere have multifarious needs
Why did Keufere converge all vital operations in his village?
Located five hundred kilometers away
How odd that workers on the spot enjoyed no advantages
Instead, they too suffered
From the delayed payment of incomes
It soon became the norm
To wait for over a year after employment
Before receiving the first salary

Oh, how badly I wanted to return
To my hometown without delay!
Yet there was no way of practicing my profession
Keufere failed to provide a conducive work environment
Even if I tried to be creative in offering minimal services
How could I succeed with regular interruptions of power?
How could I work in the absence
Of telecommunication networks?
No doubt, my education would go to waste
I would become the millionth direct underemployed victim
Of Keufere's negligence
That was causing generalized disrepair
And recurring procrastination, willfully ignoring maintenance
Leading to the perpetuation of backwardness

Keufere's mismanagement trademark was evident to all

Landscapes replete with abandoned construction sites
Sub-standard projects falling into disuse overnight
Causing shortages in the supply of basic needs and utilities
Resulting in untold damages and uncompensated losses

If one must use the possessive "his"
To describe Keufere's subjects
It begs the question:
What has Keufere done with all the wealth of the territory?
To what extent would Keufere continue to mishandle
Both the people's capacity and their resources?

I am just one of the undocumented inhabitants
Among millions posing these thorny questions,
And clamoring and beseeching for rapid change
Yet his lordship Keufere remains silent
If not, he makes promises from one generation to another,
Or takes one step ahead and two backward

Now the exploited majority are bewildered
Is his lordship Keufere deaf, indifferent, or overwhelmed?
Or is he bewitched, an *abareu**, a *ngangmirsa**, or a *nyamfuka**?

Whatever the state of mind of his highness
His despondent subjects, exposed children, vulnerable women
As much as bankrupt entrepreneurs
Not to mention jobless youth
Cannot keep on waiting

Our claim is a last-ditch effort, a distress call
To the advisers and agents of his lordship
To take immediate actions
To right the wrongs
Right now.

Abareu is the noun for "fool".

Ngangmirsa is a member of a secret society that causes people to die myste-
riously often after giving them unexpected costly gifts
Nyamfuka is a derogatory term used to describe someone who has behaved
poorly.
Each of the above terms are in common use in the Ngemba language of
Southern Cameroons.

Gossipy Journalists

Why do journalists report on the smoke
Wisping out of people's homes?
Yet ignoring roaring fires
Blazing down their very own habitations?
Why do they broadcast occurrences
In the lives of fellow citizens
As newsworthy items requiring investigations and interviews?
While bypassing fitting headline news stories
About themselves?

The assault of a female colleague's home
Became the talk of the town
Burning on the lips of youths and adults, men, and women
Students chatted about it during break,
Pondering the outcome
While *njangi** houses and *mimbo** parlors
Debated on it back and forth
Even holidaymakers from America and Europe
Thronged the newsroom
To see for themselves how despicable
The woman in question was
Whose storybook romance was under attack
By an ill-favored lady

Colleagues feared that the worse could happen
Each Monday morning
When she sat in the same editorial meeting
With both her hubby and foe
Journalists held their breath
Each time they saw the two women
Yet no one, neither the directors nor the editors-in-chief,
Included the unfolding story on the line-up for the day

Reporters listened, observed,
And indulged in gossips all day long
They saw their colleague dying gradually as if on slow poison
They commented on the unfolding drama
Like an exciting movie
They sensed the degree of burns her children suffered
They exclaimed at her 'dry' looks
But kept watching the conflagration
No one, not even the boss lifted a hand
To salvage their reputation

Finally, an opportunity enabled her to travel abroad
Colleagues regretted the vacuum her absence had created
Even then, they failed to recognize
The chance they had missed
To employ the powerful instrument
To bring solutions, to save a family
They had not taken any professional interest in her tragedy
As much as they do daily in the lives of other nationals
Or would they have preferred to publish her obituary
Highlighting impressive accomplishments
In poetic language?
God forbade it!

Njangi: a rotational savings bank for the monetary contribution of members
Mimbo: Pidgin for drink

My Pledge

According to my solemn pledge, based on our commonality
As well as the importance of the spirit
Of oneness within humanity
I declare that encouragement will be the engine of my motto
When I walk out of this trackless digression
Of my life with gusto
I pledge that my itinerary will be guided by the star of victory
Collaborating with the like-minded
In lighting up every niche in the country
With the intent of eradicating in my community
Conundrums of slackness
That have unduly enslaved my clan
Into a debilitating backwardness

My firm pledge,
Taken with the sincerity of a child, takes effect
The moment that I walk out of this body-control jacket
Emulating my parents in their rapport with acquaintances
Choosing a lifestyle of giving carte-blanche
As random chances
To the vulnerable, and the less experienced,
To arise and face challenges
Like my mother's habitual doling out
Of *Saraka** food packages
My world thus benefitting
From a surge in expressions of compassion
A practical way of standing tenaciously
Against injustice and collusion

How to honor my pledge,
Given the unforeseen, still unequipped to explain
My solid guarantee
Is that I always strive to keep my side of the bargain

And given that the current plot was concocted
To keep me in numbing pain
I cannot renege on my pledge
And expect to climb the mountain
A healing exercise, mandatory to undertake,
To avoid a fatal sprain
While releasing the energy to produce wholesome grain
The optimum investment
To ensure gain showcased in porcelain

Honoring my firm pledge
Will transform sessions of pining in vain
Into flourishing seasons of abundance of harvests,
In readiness to entertain.

Saraka is a snack party given, especially by women, to neglected children in
the village or community.

Did You Say "Released?"

The news came with a summon
To appear before the reception
Here comes, at last, my release to stroll out into celebration
My belongings returned to me in a mad rush in deportation
On the way, I decided to check my bag without obligation
Alas! while catching my first breath of redemption,
I realized in distress that my surrendered treasure
Was a mere fraction
Too late to request an investigation into the infraction
Shocked, I took a deep breath of indignation
Short of words to mock the tampering
Of a robbing guard in desperation.

"Hello, bright, beautiful, and healing sunshine!
I am released," I chanted heartily
Quickening my steps as I caught a glimpse of liberty joyfully
While the presence of freedom
Ousted my sense of loss immediately
Instant thinking of Mama's *achu*
With *njama-njama* excitedly
Baba's smile, tender kisses, and hugs for my progeny,
I imagined longingly
Propelling my return flight to my birthplace speedily
To rehearse my blunted mother tongue and Pidgin correctly
No more chains to inhibit my basking in the sun happily
No more winters to grudge nor autumns to brood inwardly

Time to celebrate the survival
Of two-score days and nine in succession
Hurray to tropical sunshine restoring interrupted circulation
Rejuvenating my being
While I dance, relax, and dine in my habitation
From sunrise to sunset, floating free like a bird in exploration.

A Dream Come True

Faith visualized herself waking up in the morning
Dressing up in the velvet sky blue costume
Of the role she had dreamed about the previous night
Walking straight up to the stage
To play the lead role
For which the Director wouldn't assign her,
For lack of name recognition and experience
Yet, she politely asked for permission
Not taking no for an answer
Then taking in a deep breath
She let the lines roll out of her
Just like the personality she represented
A voice in her cautioned,
"Quit acting if you hear persisting boos, so much for risking
If not, by all means, play on, play on
If the Director turns around and opens an inquiry on you
The stage is all yours
The cameras will fall in love with you
No wonder, with persistence, and before long,
You will become a star
For a dream is a gift to those clad in readiness
To act out the scenes cast in their minds to their heart's desire
For goodness sake, way beyond art for art's sake
In perfect alignment
With their temperament, personality, and character
Not until Faith received her crown did it dawn on her
That indeed it was a dream come true.

ACKNOWLEDGMENTS

My first gratitude goes to my Creator and Redeemer, for giving me the inspiration to zero in on the lessons of my personal life crisis, making sense of complications that rock nerves in each human being. Having overcome, I can confidently claim the promise that "all things work together for good to those that love God, and who are called according to His purpose" (Romans 8:28).

Thanks also to my friends of Golf North and Golf East at the Erie County holding center, Buffalo, New York for the moments that we lifted each other's spirit. I still recall how you, Danielle La Tore (fellow poet), Tracy Smothers, Kizzy Gamblin, Vanessa Plew, Tanja Milokovic, Filomena Montano, Eloidina Garcia, Lettie Frazier, L. Tanya Lewis, and Michelle Evans, listened to my poems night after night and encouraged me. Thanks to you, Carmen Hooser, for your remarkable kindness in time of need.

I will never forget those reassuring telephone calls you made, my compassionate friend, Antonia Agbor. Thanks also to my friend in deed, Mrs. Elizabeth Essoka, for comforting my children during the most unsettling Christmas and New Year ever, due to their mother's silence, and her inability to send them gifts and wishes while celebrations lasted.

Thanks to my family and other friends for painful interminable hours of anxiety you endured for me, your telephone calls, material support, and prayers. What consolation you brought to me, my beloved brother, Dr. Fon Ngu, and your dear wife, Frida, through your visit, driving for 600 miles approximately, each way. As for my church families, the enriching life lessons we studied together as well as the aura of love that bound us in mutual support for years, sustained me during my incarceration.

My immense gratitude to Dr. Nche Zama, whose unflinching support for my poetic art led him to insist that I was a writer, and not just a journalist. "Stop wasting your talent doing routine jobs?" he often said.

Thanks to the people and government of the United States of America for not inflicting any physical or mental torture on my person during the period when they took away my personal freedom. Also, the in-house library provided momentary relief from agony while learning something new.

Immense thanks to my sister, Manyi Ngum Delphine Zama for proof-reading the initial copy, and giving her impressions which aided in the editing process. I am grateful to my brother-in-law, Mr. Fidelis Zama Chi, who, within limited time, helped to edit and proofread, while offering key proposals in the structuring of the collection.

Thanks to everyone else that has contributed, directly or indirectly to the circumstances that have compounded to jettisoning me from the free ship of life into an unspectacular ocean of merciless waves of doing time. In the sheer struggle to keep my head above water, I was obliged to transcend myself—behold the product of an excruciating birth in your hands!

ABOUT THE AUTHOR

Photo credit: author

Mary Ngwebong Ngu is a veteran journalist, writer, and poet. She was a news anchor at Cameroon Radio Television (CRTV), and later Economic Correspondent as well as Special Correspondent at the Presidency of the Republic of Cameroon. Holder of an MA in Information & Communication Sciences from the University of Yaounde, she has written numerous articles in local newspapers and foreign magazines. Mary was a Research Officer at the Prime Minister's Office, and later, Second Councillor at the Embassy of Cameroun in Belgium. She is the author of *Earth, Breath & Touch: Inspirational Poems for the Beloved* (2001), as well as *My Foolishness Prevails* (2021), a gripping account of how she overcame a personal life tragedy. In 1993, she became one of the "Young African Leaders "within the framework of the United States Information Service-sponsored program for training on "Pluralism and Democracy."

Her second poetry book, *Escape from Prison* (2021), written during detention in the US catalogues her experiences from a prolonged period of separation from her family as well as displacement from her native community.

ABOUT THE PUBLISHER

Spears Books is an independent publisher dedicated to providing innovative publication strategies with emphasis on African/Africana stories and perspectives. As a platform for alternative voices, we prioritize the accessibility and affordability of our titles in order to ensure that relevant and often marginal voices are represented at the global marketplace of ideas. Our titles – poetry, fiction, narrative nonfiction, memoirs, reference, travel writing, African languages, and young people's literature – aim to bring African worldviews closer to diverse readers. Our titles are distributed in paperback and electronic formats globally by African Books Collective.

Connect with Us: Go to www.spearsmedia.com to learn about exclusive previews and read excerpts of new books, find detailed information on our titles, authors, subject area books, and special discounts.

Subscribe to our Free Newsletter: Be amongst the first to hear about our newest publications, special discount offers, news about bestsellers, author interviews, coupons and more! Subscribe to our newsletter by visiting www.spearsmedia.com

Quantity Discounts: Spears Books are available at quantity discounts for orders of ten or more copies. Contact Spears Books at orders@spearsmedia.com.

Host a Reading Group: Learn more about how to host a reading group on our website at www.spearsmedia.com

Printed in the United States
by Baker & Taylor Publisher Services